What Tommy Did

Guess what Tommy did when he stayed at our place.

He tried to put clothes on the dog.

My dad said, "Dogs don't like to wear clothes, Tommy."

He tried to give the cat a bath.

My dad said, "Cats don't like water, Tommy."

He put a blanket over the bird cage.

My dad said, "Birds don't like to be covered in the daytime, Tommy."

He tried to catch the fish.

My dad said, "Fish need to stay in water, Tommy."

When Tommy's parents came to take him home, he was playing the drums.

My dad said, "It's time to go home, Tommy."

Tommy's mother gave him a hug.
"Have you had a good time?"
she asked.

15

"Yes," said Tommy.
"He sure has!" said Dad.